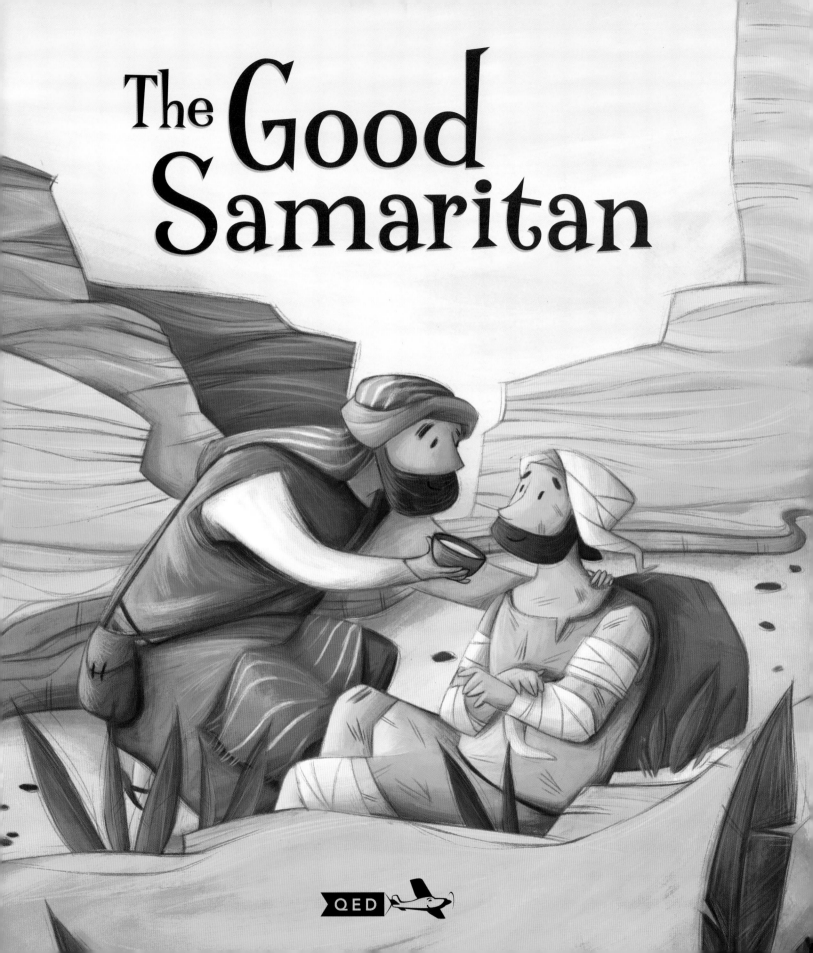

The Good Samaritan

QED

Jesus was a great storyteller. People came from miles around to hear his stories about God and his kingdom.

One day, Jesus told this story, to help people understand how God wanted them to care for one another...

"A man set off down the long road from Jerusalem to Jericho. He left the city and soon he was walking through the lonely hills.

The man felt a bit scared among the shadowy cliffs. There might be fierce wild animals living in the rocky caves.

There might be...

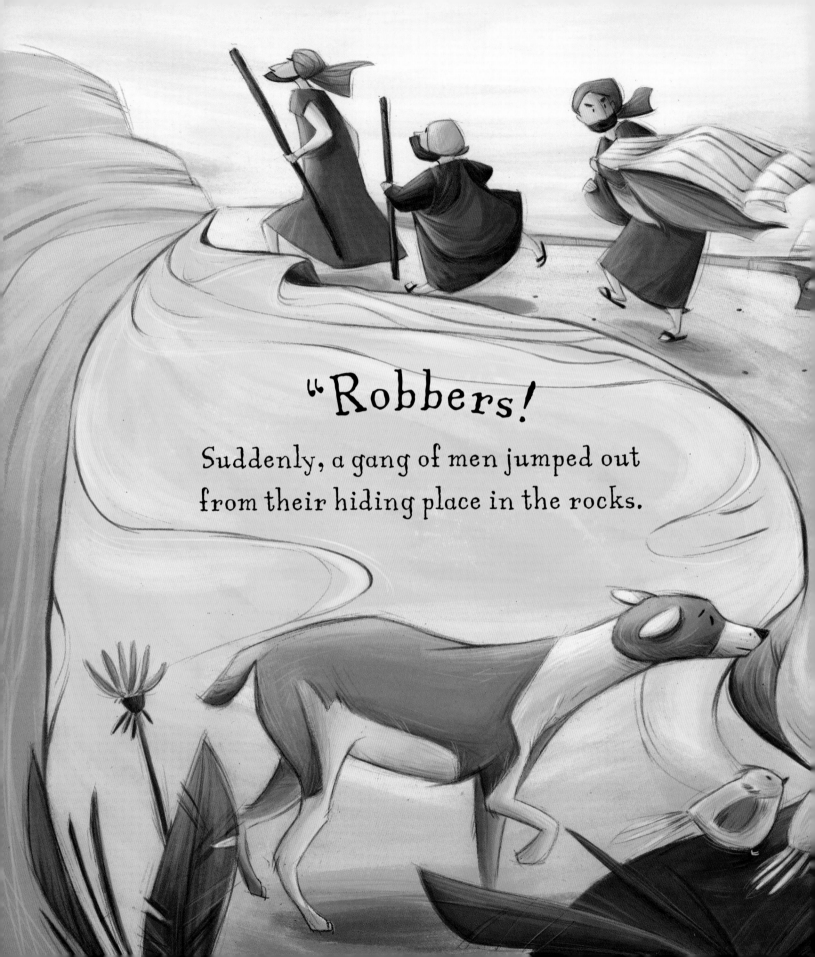

"Robbers!

Suddenly, a gang of men jumped out
from their hiding place in the rocks.

The robbers knocked the man down. BASH! They beat him up and stole all he had. Then they left the poor man lying at the side of the road.

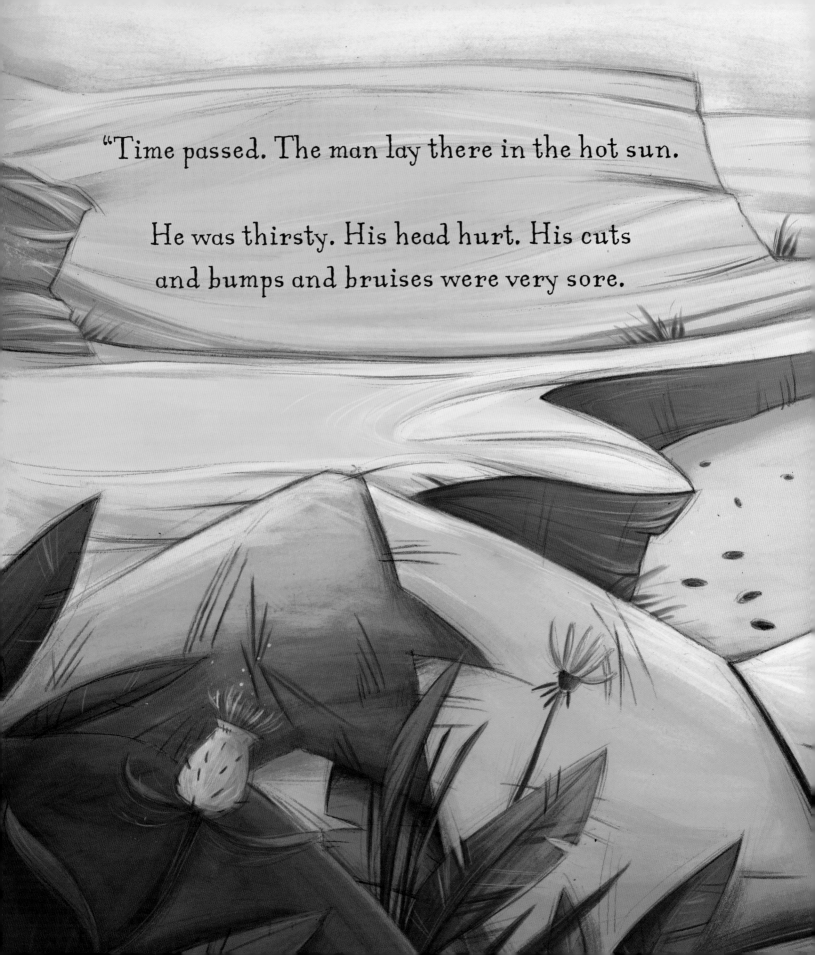

"Time passed. The man lay there in the hot sun.

He was thirsty. His head hurt. His cuts
and bumps and bruises were very sore.

The man needed help.
How long would he have to wait?

"At last, the man heard footsteps.

'Help!'

A priest from the temple in
Jerusalem came along. Surely
this man who taught about
God would stop to help?

The priest saw the man lying there but didn't go near him.

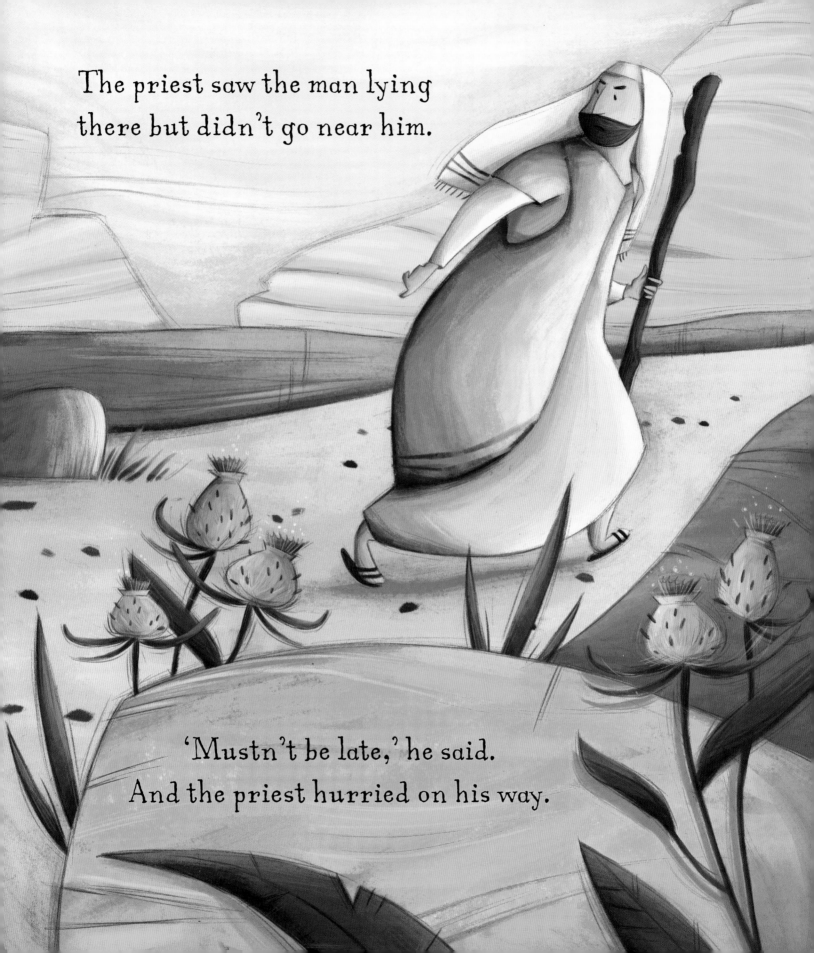

'Mustn't be late,' he said.
And the priest hurried on his way.

He crept closer to look at the man. The man told
him he had been attacked by robbers.

'The robbers might still be nearby!' he thought.

And he too went on his way.

Oh dear. It was a foreigner: a man from Samaria.
His people didn't talk to Samaritans.
They didn't like one another.

Why should this
stranger help?

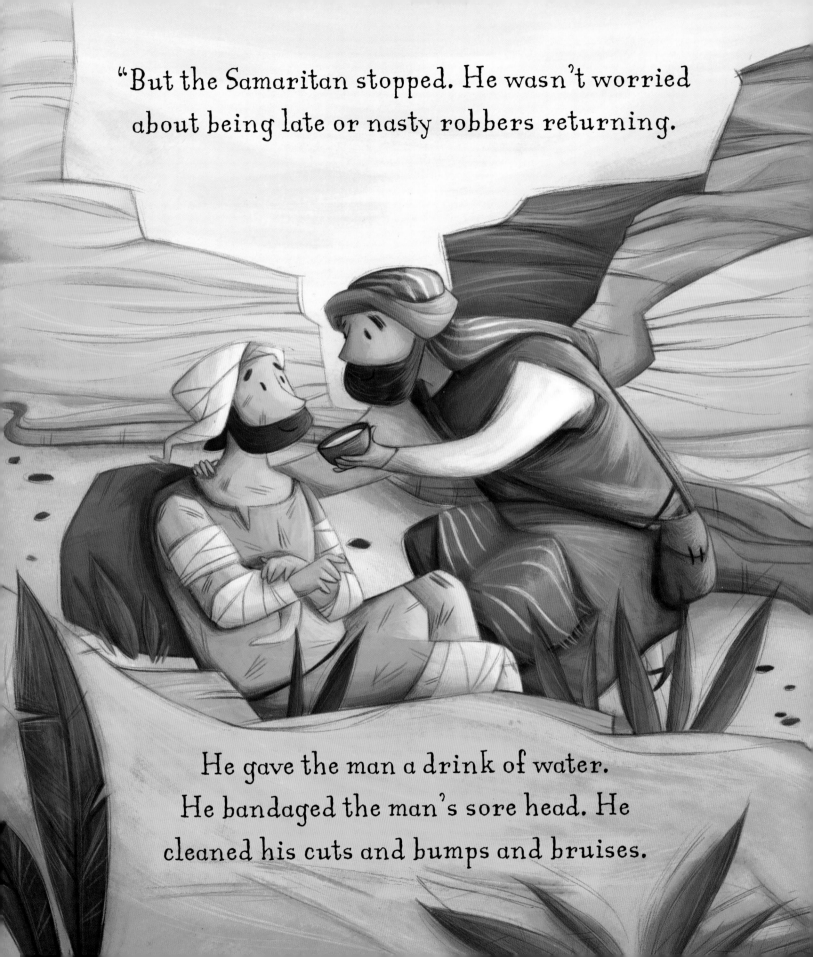

"But the Samaritan stopped. He wasn't worried about being late or nasty robbers returning.

He gave the man a drink of water. He bandaged the man's sore head. He cleaned his cuts and bumps and bruises.

Then he gently lifted him onto his donkey.

"The Samaritan led the donkey down the rocky road until they reached an inn.

'I need somewhere to care for this poor man,' he told the innkeeper. 'He has been attacked by robbers.'

"The next day, the Samaritan gave the innkeeper some money and said:

'Take care of him and let him stay. If you need more, then I will pay.'

Promising he would return,
the Samaritan went on his way."

Jesus looked at the people
listening to his story.

"So which man did what
God wants?" he asked.

"The man who showed kindness,"
someone answered.

"Now go and do the same," said Jesus.
"Show God's love to anyone who needs
your help. Even strangers."

Next Steps

What does Jesus want us to learn from the story of the Good Samaritan?

Jesus told this story to show how God wants us to treat other people. He wants us to be kind to others and to show love to anyone who needs help, just as the man from Samaria did when he stopped to help the injured traveller.

You can find this story in Luke 10 in the Bible:
"Love your neighbour as yourself" (Luke 10:27).

Now that you've read the story, here are some things to talk about and join in with.

★ Say the names of some people you love: how have you ever helped them?

★ Have you ever needed help?

★ Were you helped by a person you knew?

★ Does it make a difference whether we know the person we're helping or not?

★ Try to memorize the Samaritan's rhyme: "Take care of him and let him stay.
If you need more, then I will pay."

★ Copy the actions of the characters in the story: pretend to walk down the road; care for the hurt man; pay the innkeeper; wave goodbye.

Quarto is the authority on a wide range of topics.

Quarto educates, entertains and enriches the lives of our readers—enthusiasts and lovers of hands-on living.

www.quartoknows.com

A catalogue record for this book is available from the British Library.

ISBN 978 1 78493 838 3

Printed in China

Author: Su Box
Illustrator: Simona Sanfilippo
Editorial Director: Vicky Garrard
Designer: Victoria Kimonidou